Stories about Black History: Vol. 2

I0176512

Danita Smith

ISBN: 0-9770047-8-3
ISBN-13: 978-0-9770047-8-2

DEDICATION

This book is dedicated to our future.

NOTES

Our goal is to uplift children through education and history and to promote positive images of ourselves and others.

To that end, we release short stories about black history every month and are now releasing those stories in ebook and in paperback form.

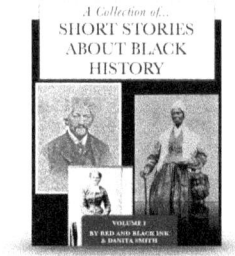

Our first volume is available only as an ebook.

Therefore, ALL of the stories from volume 1 have been included in this paperback edition.

Please visit our website for more information:

BlackandEducation.com.

CONTENTS

	Notes	ii
1	Henry Johnson and the Harlem Hellfighters (369th)	Pg 1
2	Charles Ball and the War of 1812	Pg 7
3	Ethel Waters: A Remarkable Career	Pg 11
4	Ida B. Wells and Why She Began to Write	Pg 17
5	Harriet Tubman: The Combahee River Raid (Volume 1)	Pg 27
6	Frederick Douglass: How He Learned to Read and Write (Volume 1)	Pg 33
7	Sojourner Truth and Her Famous Lawsuit (Volume 1)	Pg 41
8	Phillis Wheatley: An Example of Erudition	Pg 47
9	Benjamin Banneker: A Renaissance Man and An Abolitionist	Pg 51
10	Beginnings of the African Methodist Episcopal Church	Pg 57
11	History of Hilton Head and Mitchelville During the Civil War	Pg 63
12	William Jones and His Escape	Pg 67
13	Lewis Latimer: Inventor, Draftsman, and Electrical Engineer (Volume 1)	Pg 71
14	Biddy Mason: An American Pioneer (Volume 1)	Pg 79
15	Carter G. Woodson & Black History Month (Volume 1)	Pg 83
16	Charles Young and the Buffalo Soldiers (Volume 1)	Pg 87
	References and Credits	Pg 93
	About Us	Pg 109

1

HENRY JOHNSON
AND
THE HARLEM HELLFIGHTERS (369TH)

William Henry Johnson was born in Winston Salem, North Carolina in 1892. While still a teenager, Johnson moved to New York...he was an industrious young man and found work as a soda mixer, in a coal yard, as a chauffeur, and eventually as a redcap porter in Albany's train station.

In April of 1917 the United States declared war on Germany and, just two months later, William Henry Johnson volunteered to serve his country—he enlisted on June 5, 1917.

He was assigned to the colored 15th New York Infantry Regiment (in Company C)—an all-black National Guard unit…which would become the 369th Infantry Regiment (the "Harlem Hellfighters") of the 93rd Division, American Expeditionary Forces.

African-American units were not allowed to serve alongside white Army units, so General Pershing, commander of the American Expeditionary forces, eventually brigaded and attached this infantry regiment to French forces during the war.

The men of the 369th were given front-line combat duty on the western edge of the Argonne Forest in France.

On one occasion, the Infantry received intelligence that German forces were going to attack their position and, as a result, Private Henry Johnson and Private Needham Roberts were assigned to guard duty, at night.

It was the evening of May 15, 1918 when Johnson and Roberts were suddenly attacked…they found themselves cut off from any help and surrounded by at least twelve German raiding men.   Roberts and Johnson used all of their ammunition in the ensuing battle.

Both Roberts and Johnson were severely wounded, when Johnson noticed German soldiers pulling Roberts off and dragging him—to capture him. Johnson leapt into action.

He ran from his position, toward the men who were dragging Roberts, and struck one of them with the butt of his rifle. He then pulled out a bolo knife and struck one of the men in the head and turned around to another and struck him in the stomach. This brought Johnson some time…he fought and then lobbed grenades at the remaining enemy forces, until they withdrew. In this way, he was one of a two-person team that was able to fight off a raiding force of at least twelve men and he prevented that enemy force from capturing Needham Roberts as a prisoner of war.

The German raiding party left behind valuable evidence; including weapons and other equipment.

New York Division of Military and Naval Affairs. Sgt. Henry Johnson and the Harlem Hellfighters' parade is shown as it passes through New York during February 1919.

French officials recognized Johnson's bravery and awarded him their highest military award for valor—the *Croix de Guerre avec Palme.* Though Johnson was badly wounded, he stayed with his unit, and did not return home until the war's end.

When Johnson did return home, he had difficulty finding a job because of his wounds—during the war he sustained 21 injuries, while in various combat situations.

These injuries made it difficult for him to find steady employment and he died in 1929.

In 1996 he was, posthumously, awarded the Purple Heart and, in 2002, he was awarded the Distinguished Service Cross.

On June 2, 2015 he received America's highest military decoration, the Medal of Honor.

Arlington National Cemetery,

Henry Johnson is buried in this hallowed site.

Harlem Hellfighters

About 380,000 African Americans served in the wartime Army during World War I and approximately 200,000 of them were sent overseas. Over half of those who were sent were assigned labor duties such as building roads, bridges, trenches, etc. and 42,000 of them served in combat situations.

The 369th would be one of those units who saw combat and it would distinguish itself on the battlefield; earning the nickname the "Harlem Hellfighters" (because many of the men were from the area of Harlem).

In December of 1917, Russia and Germany came to an agreement and reached an armistice, which allowed Germany to focus more troops on the Western Front. The 369th was a part of the effort to repel this German offensive.

The 369th was assigned, as we have mentioned, to brigade with French troops (and not American troops) and on September 25, 1918, in Meuse-Argonne, the 369th was there!

Fighting alongside of French soldiers, the 369th was instrumental in that battle...sustaining heavy casualties, while facing severe opposition. They helped to capture the town of Sechault and, at one point, the 369th advanced faster and farther than their French counterparts, to the left and right of them. When they fell back to reorganize, they had advanced some 8.7 miles in the face of heavy German fighting.

This heroic effort earned the entire regiment the French *Croix de Guerre.*

New York's famous regiment arrives home from France.

National Archives and Records Administration.

The "Hellfighters" are credited with participating in the Champagne-Marne, Meuse-Argonne, Champagne 1918 and Alsace campaigns.

During the course of their service, 171 of their men and officers received medals. The 369th spent more days in combat than any other American unit during World War I—191 days.

When they came home they were greeted with a big parade in New York, but not with equality and freedom in their everyday lives.

Despite the discrimination they experienced (at home and abroad), their service cemented, in history, their contributions toward making the world "safe for democracy".

2

CHARLES BALL
AND THE WAR OF 1812

Charles Ball was born, probably in 1781....enslaved in Maryland. His grandfather was taken from Africa and Ball was the third generation of his grandfather's family to be enslaved in America.

Ball was owned by a man from Calvert County, Maryland, who also owned property in Washington, D.C. At that time (during the early 1800s), a good percentage of enslaved people, in the nation's capital, were hired out to work in the Navy Yard as seamen, cooks, and as other laborers. The men would work for a contracted period of time and their wages would be paid to their owners. Ball became one of these men.

He came to the nation's capital, where he began to work as a cook aboard the *USS Congress.*

Later on, after some dispute about who "owned" Charles Ball, Ball was awarded to Levin Ballard, Sr. and unbeknownst to Ball, Ballard decided to sell him to a southern slave trader.

Ball had no idea he had been sold—he was grabbed one morning, while working for Ballard, and placed in chains. He was taken that day across the Patuxent River, where he joined 19 other men and 32 women who had also been sold to this slave trader. The men were confined with iron collars about their necks and were handcuffed in pairs. The women were tied (and connected together) with ropes which were around their necks—they all remained in those chains and ropes, as they travelled south, for more than four weeks (over 30 days).

Ball was sold to a man in South Carolina, where he worked to harvest cotton, and he was eventually moved to Georgia. When he moved to Georgia he fell into the hands of a mean-spirited woman who was the motivation for his successful escape.

After months on the run, Ball made it back to Maryland where he came, at night, to his wife's door and nervously knocked. She could not believe it was him, and his children didn't even recognize him, because it had been seven years since he left.

Now that Ball was back in Maryland, he had to find a way to keep safe and to make money. He decided to volunteer with Commodore Joshua Barney's flotilla and to pretend to be a free man. This was around the time when the British were preparing to launch an attack on Washington via the Chesapeake Bay during the War of 1812.

As the months went on, the British did attack and Charles Ball participated in the Battle of Bladensburg in defense of Washington.

He later also joined the efforts to protect the city of Baltimore during the British assault on September 13 - 14, 1814.

The site of the Battle of Baltimore, Sept. 13 - 14, 1814—Ft. McHenry.

Charles Ball later stayed in Maryland and was able to save enough money to buy a small piece of land. His first wife passed away and he married another woman who was free. They had several children and he hoped to pass the remainder of his life, in this way, on his farm.

That hope would fade when, one day, a sheriff showed up at his home and said he had an order for Ball's arrest. It turned out that the brother of Ball's former owner was in Baltimore, to claim him as his property. There was not much that Ball could do and he was returned, enslaved, to Georgia. He immediately began to think of a way to escape again.

His first attempt failed, but he decided he would not stop trying. He was sold to another man and was kept under strict guard.

He found a way to get out of the home he was locked in, at night, and made his way to a ship in Savannah, Georgia. He was able to get on board that ship and eventually made it to freedom.

He settled outside of Philadelphia and dictated his autobiography to a lawyer, named Isaac Fisher. His autobiography, *Slavery in the United States: A Narrative of the Life and Adventures of Charles Ball, etc...*was first published in 1837. It was again published in 1858, with some revisions.

Ball's accounts of his life in slavery were used as a reference by Mark Twain when he wrote about the topic in his novel, *A Connecticut Yankee in King Arthur's Court.*

3

ETHEL WATERS:
A REMARKABLE CAREER

Ethel Waters (1896 - 1977), William Gotlieb Collection.

Ethel Waters was born at the turn of the century (in 1896) in Chester, Pennsylvania. Much has been made of her rough childhood and of her challenging upbringing, but I believe she should be remembered more for her accomplishments than for the difficult circumstances surrounding her birth.

Waters was raised by her grandmother; her mother was young when she had Ethel and Ethel's grandmother was left, mostly, to raise her.

Ethel's grandmother was a domestic worker and she often had to spend the night at her jobs, so she spent long hours away from home. Therefore Ethel (although she had aunts), grew up without much supervision.

By the time she was eight, she was working as a maid and she continued to work, off and on, for over a decade.

She also was in and out of school, as a child, but was able to stay in a catholic school for a brief period of time. At that school she was a "trouble-maker" and got into difficulties most often around lunchtime. The sisters in the school saw that Ethel often acted up at lunch and noticed that she didn't have adequate food to bring down for the meal, on many days (she often didn't have breakfast before going to school either). So, the sisters decided to give her little chores to do before lunch began.

Once those chores were done, they invited her to sit with them and to eat lunch—that way Ethel didn't feel singled-out and she felt that the food was adequate payment for the chores she completed. This was an act of kindness that Ethel never forgot...even into her older age.

Her Singing Career

One night on her birthday, which was on October 31st— Halloween, Ethel went to a club where she dared to go up and sing in front of the crowd. When she did, a couple of vaudeville managers heard her sing and convinced her to go with them to Baltimore (for $10 a week) and to try her luck out in the vaudeville circuit. Ethel was making $3.50 a week and figured she had nothing to lose; she left everything behind and went. She played in front of all-black audiences and joined a grouped called the *Hill Sisters*. Ethel was billed as "Sweet Mamma Stringbean" because of her slender frame.

Soon, she did something that would set her apart from other singers—she became the first woman to perform W. C. Handy's *St. Louis Blues*, in public. She sang it in a style that was different from the legendary Bessie Smith. Ethel was lighthearted, when she needed to be, and she would recite things musically...as well as perform songs, which was different and audiences "ate it up."

She then went to New York and began singing in nightclubs, like the Cotton Club, and actually started appearing in musicals. In 1921 she began recording music and it is thought that she was one of the first African Americans to perform on radio, in 1922.

In 1923, she auditioned for a theatre in Chicago and became one of the first successful African Americans to perform in front of all-white audiences. Others had tried, and some did so in blackface, but Ethel was among the first successful entertainers to crossover in this way.

In 1925, she recorded *Dinah* with Columbia Records—this recording was inducted, in 1998, into the GRAMMY Hall of Fame.

Two of her other recordings, *Am I Blue* (Columbia, in 1929) and *Stormy Weather* (Brunswick, 1933) were also inducted into the GRAMMY Hall of Fame.

Her 1933 version of *Stormy Weather* has also been added to the National Recording Registry of the Library of Congress. The song was originally intended to be sung by Cab Calloway —the composers, Harold Arlen and Ted Koehler, wanted Calloway to sing it at the Cotton Club revue that year, but Calloway had left and Duke Ellington replaced him. Ellington was obviously not a singer and Ethel Waters agreed to sing the song.

The crowd was electric with anticipation...many folks had heard of the song, but had not heard someone like Ethel sing it.

After her first performance of *Stormy Weather* at the Cotton Club, she received 12 encores from the audience. Later that year she recorded the song and her recording is a part of the National Recording Registry, as we have mentioned.

All-in-all Ethel Waters recorded over 250 songs and many of them became well-known in the world of music.

Acting/Theatre

Ethel's talents and theatrical flare also led her to the stage and to Broadway. She performed in plays such as *Africana, Rhapsody in Black, As Thousands Cheer,* and *Cabin in the Sky.* Her first such appearance was in the musical, *Hello 1919!.*

In 1939 she performed a dramatic role in DuBose Heyward's, *Mamba's Daughters*. She played the role of "Hagar", a strong and struggling mother who tried to prevent her daughter from being attacked. The role had all kinds of parallels to Ethel's own life, but she saw in it an opportunity to embrace larger issues. After her very first show, she received 17 curtain calls.

Television

In June of 1939 Ethel Waters became the first African American to star in her own television show. NBC had just begun regular television broadcasting, starting with the World's Fair, in April of 1939 and the company wanted to test new ideas. A program was worked out with Ethel Waters and it was called *The Ethel Waters Show*. It featured Waters, along with African-American actresses, Fredi Washington and Georgette Harvey—they performed a scene from, *Mamba's Daughters*. Other skits and performances were done and, in this way, Ethel Waters became the first African American to star in a television show— near the birth of regular television programming.

Over a decade later, in 1950, she was cast in the starring role of the situational comedy, *Beulah*. She played the title role of "Beulah", a maid. The role reinforced racist stereotypes of black women and men, for which Ethel received much criticism.

I, myself, find it difficult to admire her in such a role, but I also find it difficult to criticize her completely because she was the first to break down so many barriers that were shut to African Americans and what she had to do (and what she experienced in doing so) was likely no picnic.

Remarkably, Ethel Waters also became the first African-American woman to be nominated for an Emmy for a role she played in 1962 during an episode of the CBS show, *Route 66*. The nomination was for Outstanding Single Performance by an Actress in a Leading Role.

Many people believe that the first African American to have a starring role in a television show or program was Diahann Carroll in 1968 for *Julia* or Nat King Cole, in 1956, for the *Nat King Cole Show*, but Ethel Waters did it in 1950 and in 1939.

The Movies

Her movie career spanned from 1929 - 1959; during that time she starred in, or appeared in, at least a dozen films. Her most famous movie was *Cabin in the Sky* in 1943, where she was, again, cast in the starring role and she played opposite Lena Horne.

In 1949 she became the second African American to be nominated for an (Oscar) Academy Award for her role in the movie, *Pinky*. She was nominated for her role as "Granny", in the category of (Best) Actress in a Supporting Role.

Ethel Waters was a star during a time when African Americans were not respected as singers, actors, or entertainers by other segments of the nation, yet she broke down barriers that many black actors and entertainers freely walk through today.

4

IDA B. WELLS AND
WHY SHE BEGAN TO WRITE

IDA B. WELLS.

Ida B. Wells was born in July of 1862—her parents were enslaved in Mississippi. So, that meant she too was in enslaved. Many people may say to you that you cannot accomplish a lot when you are born into a difficult situation, but that is simply

NOT TRUE and Ida B. Wells is a great example of this!

Ida B. Wells went on to become a champion of human rights and a leading figure in the fight against lynchings in America.

She and her family were freed from slavery as a result of the Civil War. Her parents, Jim Wells and Elizabeth Warrenton, decided to stay in Holly Springs, Mississippi. Her father was a skilled carpenter and her mother was a devoted religious woman.

Jim Wells was selected as a trustee for Rust College (it was then called Shaw University) and Ida and her siblings went to school there. In fact Ida's mother, Elizabeth, went to school with her children until she learned how to read the Bible for herself.

Unfortunately, both Elizabeth and Jim died in 1878 and Ida, still a teenager, was left to care for her remaining siblings.

She got a job as a teacher and began to take care of her family. She later went to Memphis and got another position as a teacher and got help from family members and friends in caring for her siblings.

The Train Ride

When she was twenty-two years old, she boarded a train to Woodstock, TN. While on the train, the conductor came around to collect everyone's ticket, but he did not accept Ida's. Ida had a first-class ticket and was sitting in the car that matched her ticket, but the conductor told her she would have to move to another section. Ida asked, "Why?" Then she refused to get up.

The conductor then grabbed her and tried to forcibly remove her from her seat, but she held the seat in front of her and bit the back of the conductor's hand.

He then got two other men who physically took Ida from her seat and tried to put her into the smoking car of the train. She refused to go into that car and got off at the next stop. Later, she sued the company. She won her lawsuit, but the case was appealed to the state Supreme Court and the decision was overturned.

Ida began writing for a church newspaper in Memphis and the first article she wrote was about her court case. Her writings became so popular that she was eventually asked to join a local newspaper, the *Free Speech and Headlight* (later simply called the *Free Speech*)—her career in journalism was underway.

The Event That Changed Her Life

As you can see, Ida B. Wells was not a person to back down when she was treated unfairly and that characteristic would be tested when she found those she knew were being wronged as well. So, when the murders of three men she knew took place, she would not keep quiet.

Thomas Moss, Calvin McDowell and Henry Stewart all owned the People's Grocery Company in a mostly black section of town; not far away was a white-owned grocery store that also served the mostly black community. The two stores were somewhat rivals, but Moss, McDowell and Stewart were so well-liked in the community, that they didn't feel threatened, according to Ida.

On one day, a group of boys (black and white) were playing marbles and they started fighting. The father of one of the Caucasian boys was angry that his son had been beaten and decided to flog the African-American boy who beat his child. This angered some of the African-American men and they confronted that man and another fight broke out.

The man then approached the rival grocery store owner for support and this drew Moss, McDowell and Stewart into the whole affair.

The word got around that there were men who intended to "clean out" the People's Grocery Store…so, Moss, McDowell and Stewart had men stationed as lookouts in their store.

On one Saturday night, some men did come around the grocery store and the lookouts fired at them. It turns out that they were officers, but they were not there on official police business. Three of them were hit and Moss, McDowell and Stewart were arrested.

Sunday morning, police went door-to-door and arrested

over one hundred African-American men for what they called a "conspiracy."

Moss, McDowell and Stewart were in jail, while the officers recovered in the hospital. On the third night of their arrest, an angry mob gathered outside of the jailhouse.

Some members of that mob were let inside of the jail and they grabbed Moss, McDowell and Stewart, from their cells. They boarded a railroad car, in back of the jail, and took them about a mile north of the city where they shot all three of them.

That next morning, a newspaper delayed its morning edition in order to give details of the event. The newspaper reported on the abduction of the men from their jail cells…of their travel north of the city…and that Thomas Moss begged for his life—for the sake of his wife and child.

When he was asked if he had any last words, Moss reportedly replied, "Tell them (colored people) to go West." He felt that there was no justice for black people, in that city.

All of this happened while Ida was out of town, in Mississippi, and by the time she got back, Moss had already been buried. When she got back, she went through certain points in her head…

The mob was able to get Moss, McDowell and Stewart out of their cells while they were under police protection.

She must have also wondered, "Who was operating the railroad car as it travelled a mile north of the city?"

She questioned how the newspaper was able to give so many details about the event. She thought that someone from the newspaper must have been there, that night, or that they must have talked to somebody who was there.

Black people began to gather at the grocery store that Moss, McDowell and Stewart owned. A group of white men then came to the store and began shooting into the crowd and the people scattered. They then came into the grocery store and took whatever they could get their hands on and destroyed much of the store.

The creditors eventually closed the store and shortly thereafter any remaining goods were sold at an auction. In that way the People's Grocery Company ceased to exist. The *Free Speech* (the newspaper that Ida B. Wells partially owned) ran a leading story that week encouraging black people to do just what Thomas Moss told them to do…leave. The article encouraged black people to save their money and to go somewhere where their rights and property would be respected.

Hundreds of black people did leave town and made their way out West.

About six weeks after the murders two men came into the office of the *Free Speech*. They were from the railroad company and they wanted to ask a favor of the *Free Speech*. They wanted them to run an article encouraging black citizens to ride the streetcars again.

There had been a big drop in their business, recently, and they discovered that many black people were no longer riding the cars as much.

Ida inquired about what they thought was the reason for the decline and they responded that they thought black people were scared of the electricity that was now being used to operate the streetcars.

Ida told them that she didn't think it was because of the use of electricity, but that she thought it was because of the murders of Moss, McDowell and Stewart.

The men argued that the railway had nothing to do with the murders, but Ida retorted that the men who ran the railway were "southern lynchers" and that colored people believed that most of the white men of stature in the city knew about the plan to kill Moss, Stewart and McDowell. No one had been arrested, after six weeks, even though graphic details about their murders were written in newspapers and they were taken while they were in police custody.

After the men left the office, Ida wrote an article about their conversation. She then went to the two largest black churches in the city and told them about the conversation and about the impact on the streetcars. She told them to keep up the good work.

An Editorial

After awhile, Ida travelled to New York and met with her friend, T. Thomas Fortune—a well-known African-American newspaperman who helped to run several papers there, including the *New York Age*.

While she was there, she learned that the office of her paper, the *Free Speech,* had been attacked and that the equipment had been destroyed. Her friends warned her not to come back to Memphis. You see, before Ida left, she wrote an editorial. In the editorial, written in May of 1892 (three months after Moss, McDowell and Stewart were murdered), she talked about eight lynchings that had taken place since the last publication of the *Free Speech*. Since then, three black men had been killed by mobs for allegedly killing white men and five black men had been lynched for allegedly raping white women.

Ida said in her editorial that nobody believed the old lie that black men chronically raped white women and that southern white men might be surprised if they knew the true nature of these relationships. This was seen as an outrageous thing for a black newspaper to write, but Ida was speaking from the experiences she had and information she gathered while investigating actual lynchings.

Ida had recently been to Mississippi where she heard of, or directly met with, women who were thought to have been raped by black men. In each case she investigated, she found that there was evidence that a relationship existed between the man and the woman and that the men might have been lynched based on the belief that a white woman's honor had been violated. In one case a woman, who turned out to be seventeen, was found in the cabin of a black man. The newspaper reported that she was seven, not seventeen. She also met with a mother whose son had been lynched and the mother told her how her son had been involved with a young white woman and that he had been lynched after their relationship was discovered.

Ida had all of these things in mind when she wrote that editorial in May of 1892—she could not return to Memphis.

She began writing for the *New York Age* and was invited to speak on the topic of lynchings. She presented facts and information and asked people to make up their minds on their own, since the men who were lynched weren't given the benefit of trials by juries.

In her famous article, which was also published in the

1892 pamphlet, *Southern Horrors: Lynch Law in All Its Phases,* Ida B. Wells wrote:

> "It is with no pleasure I have dipped my hands in the corruption here exposed. Somebody must show that the Afro-American race is more sinned against than sinning, and it seems to have fallen upon me to do so."

5

HARRIET TUBMAN: THE COMBAHEE RIVER RAID

(A selection from volume 1)

Harriet Tubman was not only a leader in the Underground Railroad, she was also a nurse, a scout and a spy during the Civil War. She went behind enemy lines and into enemy territory, on several occasions, to collect information and to support missions.

Her contributions can best be summed up by a letter, written by General Rufus Saxton, after the war in support of her receiving a pension for her years of service:

From General Saxton to a Lady in Auburn.

March 21, 1868,

MY DEAR MADAME:

I have received your letter informing me that Hon. Wm. H. Seward, Secretary of State, would present a petition to Congress for a pension for Harriet Tubman, for services rendered in the Union Army during the late war. I can bear witness to the value of her service in South Carolina and Florida.

She was employed in the hospitals and as a spy. She made many a raid inside enemy's lines, displaying remarkable courage, zeal, and fidelity. She was employed by General Hunter, and I think by Generals Stevens and Sherman...

I am very truly yours,

RUFUS SAXTON, Bvt. Brig. Gen., U.S.A.

An example of Harriet's abilities took place in June of 1863. Harriet commanded a team of scouts who were charged with going into the areas surrounding the Combahee

River to scout out the location of explosive devices that were designed to blow up invading Union ships and to determine where enemy defenses were stationed.

Escaped slaves and African-American volunteers were among those working with her to gather this information. Harriet originally developed the idea for this raid and was first asked to lead the raid herself, but she insisted that Colonel James Montgomery be in command. Col. Montgomery was a veteran of anti-slavery fighting in Kansas and was an associate of John Brown, whom Harriet also knew.

In a report to Secretary of War Edwin Stanton, General Rufus Saxton said,

 "This is the only military command in American history wherein a woman, black or white, led the raid, and under whose inspiration, it was originated and conducted."

Sometime before the raid actually happened, Confederate lookouts and soldiers (pickets) stationed along the Combahee River sounded a false alarm about what they believed was an invasion.

So, on June 2, 1863, when Union boats did come up the river, Confederate lookouts did not immediately notify others. Based on the intelligence gathered by Harriet and her team, and on her strategic direction, Union forces executed their plans.

Two Union gunboats made their way some 25 miles up the Combahee River; successfully navigating around the explosive devices that were designed to damage their boats and disembarking at several locations. As the ships sailed slowly up the river, African-American soldiers landed and went ashore. They encountered Confederate forces that were scattered all along the river, but were successfully able to overcome these defenses.

The soldiers waved flags and sounded horns to help alert slaves that they were there to free them, then proceeded to several strategic locations to destroy Confederate supplies and capture enemy assets.

They met very little resistance as the raid was well-planned and well-executed. Plantation owners watched as soldiers disembarked the gunboats and made their way to the plantations.

Slaves, who were told to fear Union soldiers, quickly got word that they were there to save them—not to harm them. Many slaves left their work, right in the middle of doing it, and ran toward the ships.

Harriet said she had never seen such a sight, as hundreds of people ran away from their places of bondage.

"Here you'd see a woman with a pail on her head, rice...smoking in it just as she'd taken it from the fire, young one hanging on behind,…"

Union soldiers waited at the shores aboard smaller canoes, to take the freed men and women to Union boats. Harriet helped to calm people down as they rushed to get in the canoes, ensuring them that there was enough room for everybody on the boats.

Plantation homes were burned, crops were destroyed, Confederate supplies were obtained, and several warehouses were decimated. The raid was a complete success. All-in-all, well over 700 men, women and children were freed from slavery that day and not one soldier from the Second South

Carolina Volunteers was lost.

6

FREDERICK DOUGLASS: HOW HE LEARNED TO READ AND WRITE

(A selection from volume 1)

This is an excerpt from our book, *We Were Heroes*, and it reviews the manner in which **Frederick Douglass** learned to read and write. It also gives you an idea of how other people were able to keep someone enslaved…through various means and controls.

Note that Frederick Douglass was born on the Eastern Shore of the Chesapeake Bay in Maryland (not far from where Harriet Tubman was born, although they never met during their enslavement…they did, however, meet during their work to support the Underground Railroad). Frederick Douglass was given, as a "gift," to his owner's nephew and family in Baltimore when he was less than eight years old. The story picks up from there.

In Baltimore

Mrs. Auld had never owned a slave before, so the customs Frederick submitted to on the plantation were not readily followed in this house. On Colonel Lloyd's plantation, Fredrick could not look a white woman in the eye, that might be considered disrespectful. He figured out, at an early age, how to avoid getting in trouble and succumbed to the customs of bowing down his head and speaking with "bated breath" when he approached Lucretia on Colonel Lloyd's plantation.

In Baltimore, Mrs. Auld encouraged him to look up and not to hold down his face; he felt as if he was treated as a child and not as "a pig" (as he was in Captain Anthony's house). As you are aware, he had not gotten to know his mother very well and he had long been separated from his grandmother, so Mrs. Auld became a special figure in his life.

When she would sit alone in her home and read the Bible, out loud, he felt very comfortable approaching her and asking, "Can you teach me to read?"

Mrs. Auld immediately complied and before long, he was reading three and four-letter words and knew all the letters of the alphabet. She thought nothing of teaching him to read and, in fact, was very proud of the progress he made.

"Knowledge Unfits a Child To Be a Slave"

Mrs. Auld was so excited about Frederick's skills that she told her husband—she assumed that he would be supportive. Hugh Auld was surprised that his wife was so naive and was very upset. For the first time, Frederick heard an explanation of how other people were able to keep his people in bondage.

"...probably for the first time, he unfolded to her the true philosophy of slavery, and the peculiar rules necessary to be observed by masters and mistresses, in the management of their human chattels. Mr. Auld promptly forbade continuance of her instruction; telling her, in the first place, that the thing itself was unlawful; that it was also unsafe, and could only lead to mischief. To use his own words, further, he said, 'if you give a nigger an inch, he will take an ell;' 'he should know nothing but the will of his master, and learn to obey it.' 'if you teach that nigger—speaking of myself —how to read the bible, there will be no keeping him;' 'it would forever unfit him for the duties of a slave;' and 'as to himself, learning would do him no good, but probably, a great deal of harm—making him disconsolate and unhappy.' 'If you learn him now to read, he'll want to know how to write; and, this accomplished, he'll be running away with himself.'

"Very well," thought I; "knowledge unfits a child to be a slave." I instinctively assented to the proposition; and from that moment I

understood the direct pathway from slavery to freedom.”

Mrs. Auld took some time before she fully accepted the philosophy shared by her husband, but once she did, she made it her business to watch Frederick to make sure he was not reading. He recalled being in corners or quiet places, reading, when she'd come rushing toward him, in anger, and snatch a book or a newspaper out of his hand.

It takes a lot of work to keep someone oppressed and it takes an heroic effort to get out of such an oppression!

Frederick, even as a child, was about to stand up in his own way. His ingenuity and determination drove him to find other ways to learn. He would often be sent out to run errands for the family and, when he went, he would carry a Webster's spelling book in his pocket. He met other boys in the area, during his outings, most of them were Caucasian.

In the 1800s, in a big city like Baltimore, many children— black and white—were hungry. Frederick would trade bread in exchange for spelling lessons from the other children. The boys would happily comply and many of them did it for nothing at all; they simply enjoyed teaching another child how to read and spell.

Frederick was very inquisitive. He asked questions and bounced ideas about the injustices of slavery off of his playmates. He explained how he would not be free, for the rest of his life, and how they would be able to determine their own destinies when they got older. They agreed and recognized how unfair it was for their friend to be in bondage.

Even some of the workers at the shipyard would pull Frederick aside and ask him if he was a slave. They would tell him he should go north to the free states and runaway. Frederick never told them that he agreed with them because he knew of men who would ask slaves questions about escaping, then tell their owners of the slave's desire to run away—so he kept those feelings to himself.

On August 21, 1831 Nat Turner led his rebellion in Virginia. Fredrick was only 13 or 14 at the time, living in Baltimore—having just learned fully how to read. Talk of Turner's rebellion was on the lips of many people around the country and the idea that somehow things were going to change, was imbedded in Frederick's heart. He overheard Hugh Auld speaking about "abolitionists," when people came over for dinner.

After hearing about these things, Fredrick was focused on learning anything he could about how he might become free. He looked up the word, abolition, in the dictionary, but that didn't explain to him the movement that was happening in the country. He then found a copy of a newspaper which had articles on the abolitionist movement in the North and he was further encouraged that something was going to happen because, he figured, the whole world knew about the horrors of slavery.

But what could he do to bring about his own freedom? He continued to study, and to talk to whomever he felt it was safe to talk to, in order to gather more information about abolitionism. He came across a book entitled *The Columbian Orator*, by Caleb Bingham.

This was a book commonly given to school children at that time. It provided tips on how to speak effectively, in public, and contained examples of speeches and of other fictional stories. He resolved that he would study this book and learn all that he could to increase his knowledge.

He came upon a section of the book that described a conversation between a slave and his owner, where the slave was able to give elegant reasons for his freedom to be given to him. The story ends with the owner granting the enslaved man his freedom because for every reason he could give for keeping him enslaved, the man had an effective response for why he should be free. Fredrick hoped that one day he would share in that fictional slave's experience.

Frederick continued his drive toward learning; not only did he get other children to help him and made it a point to collect various types of reading material on his own, he also decided to learn how to write. He was remarkably resourceful in his efforts.

Hugh Auld owned a ship yard in Baltimore and Frederick often had to go there and perform tasks like watching the yard while others were away on breaks. When the workers cut long pieces of wood to build the ships, they had to have a way of making sure the right pieces were delivered to the right sections of the ship. They wrote letters on the pieces of timber—"L" for larboard, "S" for starboard, etc. Frederick would go, while the carpenters were at lunch, and copy the letters they wrote down, in order to teach himself how to write.

He didn't stop there. He also went up to the boys he would meet on the street, and with a piece of chalk, he would write the few letters he knew on the pavement and say, "Beat that if you can!" The boys would write other letters, and words, with the chalk and Frederick learned more letters that way.

Frederick also slept in a loft in the Auld's kitchen and at

night he would copy passages from the Bible and a Methodist hymn book he obtained. To say the least, he was resourceful.

Frederick Douglass went on to become a very dynamic speaker and a strong abolitionist in the movement against slavery…he also wrote one of the most famous autobiographies in history, *Narrative of the Life of Frederick Douglass*.

He named real people and real places in his book because some of his critics argued that he was far too intelligent to have ever been a slave.

7

SOJOURNER TRUTH AND HER FAMOUS LAWSUIT

(A selection from volume 1)

Sojourner Truth sold pictures of herself at lectures. The caption in the above picture reads, "I sell the shadow to support the substance."

In July of 1826 **Sojourner Truth** simply walked away from slavery, with her youngest child. She didn't run...she didn't go very far...she simply decided she wasn't going to be a slave anymore.

Some years earlier the New York state legislature passed two laws, gradually emancipating slaves. The laws essentially provided that all adult slaves would be set free on July 4, 1827 and any child, born after a certain date, to an enslaved mother, would have to work for the mother's owner until the age of 21—at which time the child would also be free.

Sojourner's owner had promised her he would set her free one year before the 1827 date. When she approached him about his promise, he changed his mind; saying that she had hurt her hand (some time earlier) and did not give him the proper amount of work. So, Sojourner decided to leave...after she spun about 100 pounds of wool, she got up at dawn and walked away with her youngest child.

She did not go very far and was able to secure her freedom, which allowed her to stay in the area, however, sometime before she left, her owner sold off her youngest son, Peter, to a man named Dr. Gedney.

Gedney took Peter to New York City, with the intention of going to England, but Peter was only five years old and Gedney found him too young too suit his needs. He therefore sold Peter to his brother, Solomon Gedney, who turned around and sold Peter to his brother-in-law, in Alabama.

When Sojourner found out that her son had been sold to Alabama, she knew exactly what that meant! If Peter was not in the state of New York, he would never be emancipated at the age of twenty-one...he would be forever enslaved.

Sojourner set out to get him back, the only way she could, through the law.

Determination and God's Promise

Sojourner initially got help from a group of Quakers who instructed her to go down to the courthouse and to present her case to the grand jury. She prayed to God and asked that God help her. Armed with that faith, she set out for the courthouse.

She had never been inside a courthouse before and did not know what a grand jury really was. Once she found the right room, she presented her case in such a convincing manner that one of the jurors asked her to step into a room. There she was asked to restate her case and to swear that the child was actually hers. She was given a document to take to the local constable, in order to serve Solomon Gedney.

Solomon Gedney then secured legal counsel and was advised to go get Peter or face possible jail time. Gedney left for Alabama and months passed before he returned with Peter.

When he did return, he claimed Peter as his enslaved property and Sojourner was told that she would have to wait another several months before the matter could be addressed in court.

Sojourner did not believe she should have to wait. She believed God would answer her prayers completely and she did not want Peter to be in the custody of Gedney for another several months. Who knows what Gedney might do to him?

Her lawyer told her that she should be thankful for all they had been able to do—it was remarkable that her son was back in New York and that she should wait patiently for the next court session.

Sojourner was not satisfied...she walked around town,

wondering what she could do, when a stranger who knew of her case, approached her. He told her to go see a lawyer, named Demain, who would surely help her, if she insisted.

Faith and Effort

She went directly to Demain's house and laid out her situation. He agreed to help her and told her if she would give him five dollars, she would have her son in 24 hours. Demain was going to hire a man who "specialized" in getting things done and he needed the five dollars to pay him.

Sojourner explained that she did not have any money and had never owned a dollar in her life. She decided to ask the Quakers, who originally helped her, for assistance. She immediately left Demain's house, walked ten miles to their location, and was able to collect money from them.

She then walked back to his house and gave him all of the money she collected—a sum greater than five dollars. People wondered why she didn't keep some of the money for herself (because she was poor), but she said she only wanted her son (not the money) and she figured that "If five dollars would get him, more than that would surely get him."

She now had to wait. After a considerable amount of time passed (about 24 hours) Demain came to get Sojourner to tell her that her son had indeed been obtained and was down at the courthouse, but that he was denying that he had any family, or a mother, in this place. She had to go identify him.

She went down to the office, but when she got there, her son screamed and grabbed the leg of Solomon Gedney...claiming that Gedney was his master and that he didn't want them to take him.

Peter had a big scar on his forehead and when he was asked how he got it, he claimed that a horse in Alabama kicked him. He also had a scar on his cheek, which he said he got from running into a carriage.

The judge made Peter talk directly to him and asked him to stop looking at Gedney, when he answered.

Demain, the lawyer, began to argue that the child must be able to be claimed because his sale, out of the state of New York, was illegal under the emancipation laws and that Solomon Gedney should be fined and prosecuted.

Sojourner sat in the corner, while all of this was going on, barely breathing...thinking that if she could only get her son...she didn't care about anything else.

The judge finally declared that her son be given to her "having no other master, no other controller, no other conductor, but his mother."

A Mother's Love

When Sojourner and the other people there were finally able to calm Peter down, she looked at him and from the top of his head to the soles of his feet, he had scars all over his body. His back was whelped and looked "like her fingers, as she laid them side by side."

"How did you bear this?" she exclaimed. Peter said the scars were from the man in Alabama who had kicked, beaten, and whipped him. He said that there was also a woman, named Phillis there, who had a newborn baby. She was beaten to the point where both blood and milk ran down her body. Sojourner was horrified…she couldn't believe her son was with such an abusive man. She was able to secure her son's freedom and, in doing so, she was among the first African-American women, in the United States, to win a lawsuit.

8

PHILLIS WHEATLEY:
AN EXAMPLE OF ERUDITION

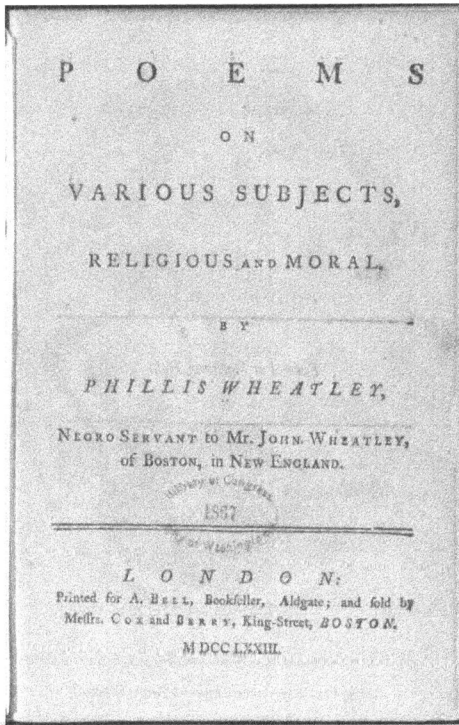

Phillis Wheatley was the fist African American to publish a book of poetry in the colonies—she lived before, during and through the American Revolution, from about 1753(?) to 1784.

The Middle Passage

Her story began in Africa where she was born. She was kidnapped when she was just seven or eight years old and placed on a slave ship. Imagine what it must have been like for her to be captured at such a young age and taken, probably by grown men, aboard a slave ship to America.

She was put on the slave ship the *Phillis* and experienced the Middle Passage through the eyes of a young child—about 25% of the enslaved Africans on that ship died before the boat reached New England.

Erudition and Learning

She arrived in Massachusetts in July of 1761 and was purchased by John and Susanna Wheatley. John Wheatley was a merchant in Boston.

They named her after the slave ship she was brought on and their last name, Wheatley, was adopted...so she eventually became known as Phillis Wheatley in her writings.

Phillis showed an interest in writing, early, and the Wheatley's supported her talents. She did not receive a formal education, but the support the family gave her in literature, Latin, and the Bible helped her develop.

She was able to do what many women were not able to do in the 1770s...she became an author.

John Wheatley wrote in a letter, dated November 14, 1772, of her talents and abilities:

> *"Phillis was brought from Africa to America; in the Year 1761, between Seven and Eight Years of Age. Without any Assistance from School Education, and by only what she was*

taught in the Family, she, in sixteen Months Time from her Arrival, attained the English Language, to which she was an utter Stranger before, to such a Degree, as to read any, the most difficult Parts of the Sacred Writings, to the great Astonishment of all who heard her.

As to her Writing, her own Curiosity led her to it; and this learnt in so short a Time, that in the Year 1765, she wrote a Letter to the Rev. Mr. Occom, the Indian Minister, while in England".

Phillis Wheatley also studied Latin and by the time she was about fourteen years old she published her first poem in a Rhode Island newspaper, the *Newport Mercury*, entitled: *"On Messrs Hussey and Coffin,"* in 1767.

A Brilliant Move

Phillis also wrote poems about famous religious and colonial leaders, of that time. Her letter and poem to George Washington drew a response from him of thanks and respect for her talents.

She often wrote poems (elegies) about prominent leaders who died. This was a brilliant move, by her, since poems of this nature...written by a woman in slavery in the 1700s...might generate a good deal of interest and attention.

For instance she wrote a work entitled:

"An Elegiac Poem On the Death of that celebrated Divine, and eminent Servant of Jesus Christ, the Reverend and Learned Mr. George Whitefield".

George Whitefield was a well-known Methodist minister who travelled through, and to, the American colonies. He was also the personal chaplain of a Countess in England—the Countess of Huntingdon, Selina Hastings. Mrs. Hastings, after this poem, took a personal interest in Phillis.

In 1773 Phillis travelled to London, with the Wheatley's son, hoping to meet Mrs. Hastings, but they were unable to meet in person. Mrs. Hastings did, however, support Phillis and in September of 1773 she helped Phillis publish her first book, *Poems on Various Subjects, Religious and Moral.*

This became the first published book of poetry by an African-American, in the colonies, and the friends she made in England encouraged John Wheatley to free Phillis later on that year.

Phillis Wheatley did not become a rich woman and her second volume of poetry was never published. She married John Peters, a free African-American man and they had three children, two of whom died early in life.

Phillis Wheatley left a legacy of erudition and dedication that should be remembered by children today.

9

BENJAMIN BANNEKER: A RENAISSANCE MAN & AN ABOLITIONIST

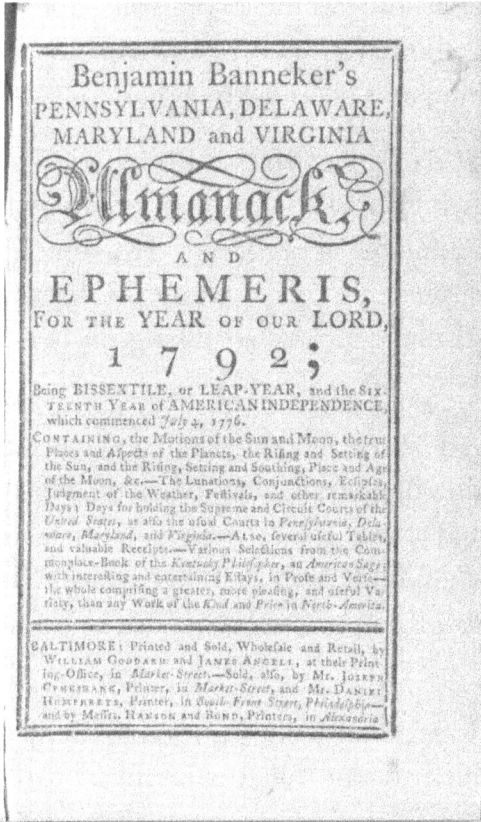

Benjamin Banneker was born on November 9, 1731 in what is today Baltimore County, Maryland.

According to accounts his grandmother, Molly Welsh, was a white English woman who was sent to the American colonies as an indentured servant.

After serving her indentured time, she was able to obtain her own property—which was a remarkable thing for a woman to do in the late 1600s. She then purchased enslaved people to work her land...she ended up buying two human beings—one of whom was said to be the son of an African king, whose name was Bannaka.

Molly freed both of the people she bought and married Bannaka. Bannaka was described as a dignified and upstanding man and he and Molly had four daughters.

Their first daughter, Mary, also married a man who was born in Africa—Robert. He was kidnapped in Africa and brought to America, as a slave. He somehow secured his freedom, adopted the first name, Robert, when he was baptized, and married Mary—taking on her last name, now spelled Bannaky.

Robert and Mary Bannaky had four girls and one son— their only son, Benjamin, was born on November 9, 1731. Robert Bannaky was a very resourceful farmer and father and, when Benjamin was just five years old, Robert used 7,000 pounds of tobacco to purchase one hundred acres of land.

Wisely, Robert Bannaky put young Benjamin's name on the deed, which meant that Benjamin (and his sisters) would most likely not be forced into slavery (and they never were) because their mother, Mary, was born free and their family (Robert and Benjamin) were registered landowners. This was a very smart move by Robert Bannaky.

Early Accomplishments

Benjamin Banneker was a self-taught man (although he

probably received some instruction in reading from his grandmother, instruction in astronomy from his father, and some education in arithmetic during his brief stay in school).

Benjamin fell in love with reading, mathematics, literature and any number of subjects. He took as much time as he could to study, in between the time it took for him to run his farm.

When Benjamin was about twenty-one years old, he came across a pocket watch which was a novel gadget at that time.

He was so intrigued by the device that he examined it...studied its inner workings...and created a fully functioning clock, made completely out of wood. This accomplishment obviously took mechanical engineering and mathematics to complete.

The clock, created in 1752, was the first of its kind in America and it kept accurate time for decades.

Banneker also corresponded with mathematicians...some of whom sent him difficult mathematical problems to solve— he would reply with an answer and, in return, send them problems to solve as well.

Banneker, as you can see, was a skilled mathematician— using his calculations he correctly predicted a solar eclipse which occurred in 1789; contrary to the predictions of other well-known mathematicians.

When he met George Ellicott, who was himself a trained mathematician, Banneker and George developed a lifelong friendship. The two spent hours delving into mathematical subjects and discussing the current events of the day. George had a great deal of respect for Benjamin's abilities and he gave Benjamin books, drafting tools, and other equipment.

Washington

In 1791 Andrew Ellicott, a relative of George Ellicott, headed up a team responsible for surveying the new Federal District Territory (which would become Washington, D.C.). George recommended that Benjamin be assigned to the team. This presented Banneker with an opportunity to work with some of the most advanced surveying equipment, of that time. The team's job was to survey the ten square-mile area by establishing its boundaries, setting up markers and determining the main streets for the city. Pierre L'Enfant was responsible for designing the city, but Ellicott's team arrived before L'Enfant and began surveying.

Banneker, who was hired as Andrew Ellicott's assistant, was responsible for many things; including maintaining the astronomical clock used in the surveying. He had to regularly monitor the rate of the clock by reading the position of the sun in the sky.

Benjamin Banneker was a part of the team that surveyed the nation's capital, long before any of its famous monuments were built.

All of this experience, and his lifelong studies, led him to also produce almanacs. Almanacs were very important resources, at the time, because they provided valuable information about the weather, the rising and setting of the sun, tides, and a whole host of other information. Benjamin Banneker published his first almanac in 1792, his series was called *Benjamin Banneker's Pennsylvania, Delaware, Maryland and Virginia Almanack and Ephemeris, for the Year of Our Lord 1792.*

Abolitionist

Banneker's accomplishments were remarkable when you consider they all took place before, during, and after the Revolutionary War…imagine being a black person and being a mathematician, an author, a farmer of your own land, an astronomer, a naturalist, and a surveyor of what would become the nation's capital, in the 1700s…in America.

On August 19, 1791, Benjamin Banneker wrote a letter to then secretary of state, Thomas Jefferson.

In his letter, Banneker asked Thomas Jefferson to remember the words,

"We hold these truths to be self-evident, that all men are created equal;…"

He told Jefferson that it was pitiable that although he had been convinced of the goodness of God in granting everyone equal privileges and rights, that he would at the same time enslave by fraud and violence so many of Banneker's brothers.

This was a remarkable thing for a black man to do in 1791 —to write such a letter. He intended only to send Thomas

Jefferson a copy of his almanac, before it was published, but the evils of slavery so weighed upon his heart that he could not help but write those words as well. He asked Jefferson to put himself in the shoes of enslaved men and women and to remove any prejudices he may have toward them.

Benjamin Banneker died in October of 1806 and long after his death his accomplishments were used as arguments against the institution of slavery.

10

BEGINNINGS OF THE AFRICAN METHODIST EPISCOPAL CHURCH

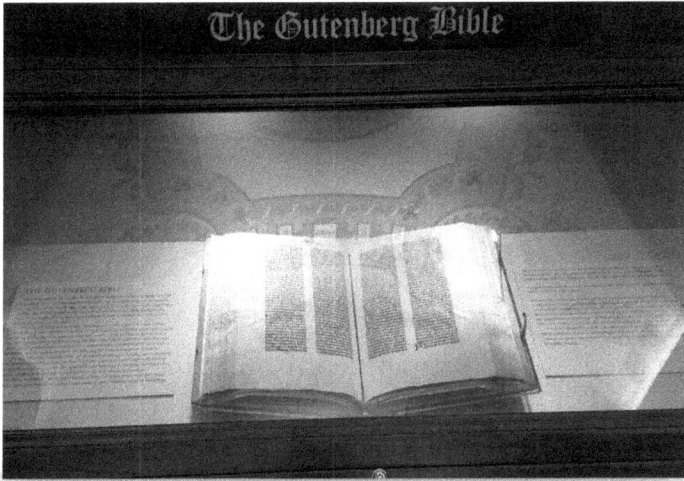

In some ways the beginnings of the African Methodist Episcopal Church can be found in the life of Richard Allen, but this is really a much larger story about people who chose to stand up and worship in a way that was seated in freedom and rooted in independence.

Richard Allen was born in slavery, in Philadelphia, in February of 1760 and he and his family were sold into Delaware. When Richard became older he and his brother began attending Methodist meetings. He convinced his owner to allow a preacher to speak in their home and as a result, his owner began to question slavery and to believe that his owning slaves made him wrong in the eyes of God...so he let Richard and his brother buy their freedom.

After working at any job he could find, Allen continued in his devotion to God and was licensed to preach. He began traveling in Delaware, New Jersey and Pennsylvania on the Methodist circuit. In 1786 he came to St. George's Methodist Church, in Philadelphia, where he was asked to preach an early morning service for black churchgoers.

Allen also organized prayer meetings and proposed that blacks in the city of Philadelphia build a place of worship to call their own, but he was met with much opposition—only Absalom Jones, William White and Dorus Ginnings agreed with him.

An Impetus

An event would happen that would 'force their hands.' It was suggested that a gallery be built, in St. George's, given the increased amount of black and white church members (which caused some tension in the church). One Sunday, as Allen and others arrived at church, they were told to go to the gallery to sit. They assumed that they would be sitting above the seats where they usually sat. As they got to their seats, the elder said, "Let us pray." Before long, Richard Allen heard a trustee speaking to Absalom Jones, pulling him up off of his knees and saying, "You cannot kneel here."

Absalom said, "Wait until prayer is over." The trustee said, "No, you must get up now." He then called over another man to help him and that man grabbed William White, to pull him off of his knees.

By this time, prayer was over and Richard Allen, Absalom Jones, William White and others got up and left the church as a body.

They knew they now had to find a place to worship of their own. They began the process of raising the money for a new church.

They were told that if they didn't stop their efforts, they would be kicked out of the Methodist connection. This did not stop them, this is remarkable because this was only several years after the end of the Revolutionary War and there was no roadmap for them to follow.

They held services on their own and when the time came for them to decide what denomination to unite with, many decided to join the the Episcopal denomination.

(This group started the African Episcopal Church of St. Thomas and eventually Absalom Jones became the first African-American Episcopal Priest).

Richard Allen, and those who wanted to remain in the Methodist tradition, went on to build their church and in 1794, their church was dedicated.

Allen later recalled some of the challenges they faced.

He and the members of Bethel were told, by a man they knew, that they should sign their new church over to the Methodist Conference (the white conference of Methodist elders, bishops, ministers, etc...) in order to be a part of the organization. They objected—they did not want to hand over ownership of their church, "They can deny us their name, but they cannot deny us a seat in heaven!" This "Mr. C." then told them that they should at least get incorporated and that he would draw up the paperwork, for them, and they agreed.

The African Supplement

For years they worked under this incorporation—some of the time it was good, some of the time it was not so good. One day an official showed up and asked to see their books and demanded the keys to the church. He said he was in charge and was the elder and that the church was not theirs, it belonged to the Methodist Conference.

The members of Bethel were flabbergasted. They went to a lawyer to inquire about this and the lawyer told them, it was true—they had been duped, and that the only way to amend their agreement was to have a two-thirds majority vote. Richard Allen then called together his society and they unanimously voted to add an alteration, called the "African Supplement."

The trustees of St. George's were not happy.

They called a meeting and demanded that Bethel pay $600 a year for their services, but Bethel would not budge. The Trustees at Bethel then agreed to a lower sum, but finally decided that $100 a year was enough.

The leadership at St. George's decided not to preach at Bethel for some time and other difficulties arose when additional preachers, outside of St. George's, began to interact with Bethel.

Leaders in the Methodist community began to publicly disown them. An elder, then, came to Bethel and told them that he would be taking charge of the congregation.

Allen and the trustees disapproved, but the elder stated that, "He did not come to consult with Richard Allen or other trustees, but (came) to inform the congregation, that…next Sunday afternoon, he would come and take…spiritual charge."

Next Sunday arrived and when he came into the church, the people were ready…a preacher from Bethel was already in the pulpit—setting up what would be a difficult showdown. As the elder approached the front of the church, the aisles were filled with churchgoers and he could not get more than halfway down any of the aisles.

This happened twice—all of these actions led to court cases to determine whether the Methodist Conference had any control over the Bethel congregation. The Pennsylvania Supreme Court determined that the Methodist Conference did not have control…this opened new pathways for the original members of Bethel.

The African Methodist Episcopal Church was formed in 1816, becoming the first independent, African-American denomination in the country.

11

HISTORY OF HILTON HEAD AND MITCHELVILLE DURING THE CIVIL WAR

Just prior to the Civil War, Hilton Head consisted of about 20 working plantations—mostly populated by enslaved men and women. The Gullah people, as you may know, were forced to come to the United States from rice-growing areas in Africa specifically for their skills in growing rice...as rice, cotton and indigo were the main crops in the lowland areas along the southeast coast of the U.S.

Because of the isolation of the sea islands along the coast of South Carolina, Georgia, Northern Florida and some parts of North Carolina...the people who were forced into slavery there developed their own distinct culture. In fact many of the people who owned those plantations, did not live on them in Hilton Head. They hired overseers and few visitors came to the island (compared to the amount of traffic that might take place in a city like Charleston, SC).

So, the people on the sea islands maintained many of their traditions from Africa and developed a creole language that is not that dissimilar from some of the creole languages that developed in Haiti and in Jamaica (and some of the other nations of the Caribbean). They continued their tradition of making baskets from the grass that grew around marshes and some of the words that have been introduced into the English language, from Africa, are attributed to the Gullah people.

Early during the Civil War, the Union decided to blockade Confederate cities to prevent supplies from coming in from Europe. In November of 1861, Union forces launched an attack along the northern border of Hilton Head Island near Port Royal Sound. Within hours, the main fort on the island had been surrendered and Union forces gained control over an important area that would become their base for blockading other areas in the South. Beaufort and St. Helena Island also fell a short time after.

Thousands of enslaved men and women were freed in the areas of Beaufort, Hilton Head, and St. Helena, as plantation owners (and their families) fled the area.

By December of 1861, there were hundreds of emancipated people in the Union encampment at Hilton Head and many more were about to make their way to the camp.

General Ormsby Mitchel ordered a village to be built that would house the increasing number of formerly enslaved people and the town of Mitchelville was born. There was a military supervisor appointed for the town, but the people of Mitchelville constructed their own homes and established their own government.

They elected a city council and created laws, or ordinances. Taxes were collected, as the people worked to support Union forces and were hired to do many tasks. The town also established sanitary regulations, punished violations of its ordinances, compensated its municipal officials and established a way to settle property and other disputes. In short, they performed all of the governmental and administrative tasks needed to run a town that grew to hold more than 3,000 people.

The people of Mitchelville also created and administered the first compulsory education law in South Carolina, which required that all of their children attend school on a daily basis. These were remarkable achievements given the fact that they were all subject to the horrors of slavery, only a short time earlier.

In 1868, Union forces left Hilton Head, which had a devastating effect on the economy and on the jobs that were a part of the livelihood of many of its residents.

Mitchelville is a somewhat forgotten part of history, now, that we should really remember.

If you're ever in Hilton Head, drive by the airport...down Beach City Road and you will be driving through history!

12

WILLIAM JONES AND HIS ESCAPE

In April of 1859, William Jones boxed himself in a crate to escape slavery. He was owned by a man who operated a grocery and William hated the idea of being enslaved. He decided to do something about it; he made sure a friend had the bill of lading and the receipt and had someone seal him inside of a box.

William was mailing himself from Baltimore to Philadelphia. The ordeal took 17 hours and William was shipped via steamboat.

While in the box, he couldn't straighten himself out and he was tested to his very limits. He was so cramped that he began to ache and was so uncomfortable that he almost yelled, but he couldn't give away his secret.

He then began to feel faint and sick, but he was able to

hold himself together. Then he began to get extremely cold and tried to keep warm, before he actually fell asleep. After many hours he reached Philadelphia on board the steamboat.

It was Sunday morning and most people did not do any work on Sundays. William's friend (who had the receipt) was expecting him and he was determined not to let William spend another day in that box.

His friend hired a carriage and went down to the wharf with the bill of lading and the receipt. He also knew where the box was located on the steamboat. When his friend reached the boat and handed the worker the bill of lading, the worker told him, "No, we don't deliver freight on Sunday." William's friend did not want to seem too anxious, but he would not give up.

Finally, the worker asked him if he would recognize the box if he saw it. William's friend said, "I think I should."

He looked around for a while and said, "I think that is it."

The worker read the directions and checked the bill of lading and said, "That is right, take it along."

William's friend was very happy that he had the box, but he now had another problem—the box was too big for the carriage...so he had to find another way to transport it. It took him an hour and a half to find a furniture "car" that could carry something that size.

He then lifted the box to put it into the vehicle, but William coughed! This startled the friend and he dropped the box and walked away so that no one would know what was inside—singing a song as he walked away to let William know everything was going to be alright.

He then came back to the box and lifted it, again, this time into the vehicle. The driver did not know what was going on and simply drove to the address he was given.

Once inside William's friend opened the box and William came out! They were overjoyed!

Members of the Vigilance Committee (a group of citizens who helped escaped slaves while they were passing through their city) were also present.

The group celebrated for hours. William made it all the way to Canada, but before going there, he stayed in Albany for a while and wrote a letter from Albany to the Vigilance Committee in Philadelphia...thanking them for their help.

This is just one example of the many ways men and women fought to end their enslavement and he wasn't the only person to do this.

13

LEWIS LATIMER: INVENTOR, DRAFTSMAN, AND ELECTRICAL ENGINEER

(A selection from volume 1)

Lewis Latimer was born on September 4, 1848 in Chelsea, Massachusetts. Just six years earlier his parents, George and Rebecca Latimer, escaped from slavery.

Lewis was the youngest of their four children; he attended school early in his life and had a thirst for education. The Civil War started when Lewis was just twelve years old (almost thirteen). His two older brothers enlisted in the Union Army and when Lewis was sixteen, in 1864, he volunteered to serve.

He joined the U.S. Navy and served on board the USS Massasoit, which was a gunboat that saw action along the James River in Virginia. The Civil War ended in 1865...Lewis Latimer was honorably discharged and then returned to Massachusetts.

In 1868 he got a job in a law firm in Boston, MA...the firm specialized in patents. He continued his commitment to furthering his education and studied the draftsmen around him. By doing this, he taught himself how to create patent drawings. He mastered the art and was promoted to the title of draftsman in the firm.

The Telephone

During this time a slew of inventions were being developed and there were many races and competitions to submit inventions before another person could get their application to the patent office.

This competitive environment, and his position in the law firm, gave Lewis Latimer a great deal of experience with the process of submitting patents. Alexander Graham Bell met Lewis Latimer while Latimer was working at the law firm. He asked Latimer if he would help him with the submission of his new invention—the telephone.

Bell and Latimer worked late nights doing the necessary work for the submission of the patent. Latimer helped draw up the blueprints and his expertise and experience in patent submissions helped Alexander Graham Bell submit his patent for the telephone just hours before a competitor submitted a similar patent.

Electrical Lighting

In 1880, Lewis Latimer went to work for the U.S. Electric Lighting Company in New York. There he became more familiar with electricity and lighting and worked with the well-known inventor, Hiram Maxim. In 1884, Latimer went to work for the Edison Electric Light Company.

There he was a draftsman, an electrical engineer, and a legal expert who was in charge of the company's library and served as an expert witness in legal cases involving the company.

In 1890 he wrote Incandescent Electric Lighting: A Practical Description of the Edison System, which explained in layman's terms, how this new electrical system worked. He later became a member of the Edison Pioneers, a group of former Edison employees—he was the only African-American member of this well-respected group.

In his lifetime, Lewis Latimer had many noteworthy accomplishments.

His most famous accomplishment was the invention of a process that improved the manufacturing of long-lasting carbon filaments (this helped to advance commercial lighting).

He also oversaw the installation of outdoor electrical lighting systems in major cities such as Montreal, New York, and Philadelphia and he wrote the first book (that was published in the U.S.) which clearly explained Thomas Edison's electrical lighting system.

Latimer, as we have mentioned, also helped Alexander Graham Bell draw up the patent for the telephone and he was a veteran who served during the Civil War.

Lewis Latimer helped to oversee the installation of early outdoor electrical systems in cities like New York, Montreal and Philadelphia.

He had two daughters with his wife Mary Wilson, whom he married in 1873. Lewis Latimer was an American who truly contributed to the advancement of his society. The most amazing part of his story, however, begins with his mother and father.

George and Rebecca Latimer

George and Rebecca Latimer were enslaved in Norfolk, Virginia and, on October 4, 1842, they escaped. Rebecca was pregnant and she was determined not to have her child (or any of their children) born into slavery. George was very fair-skinned (his father was the brother of his owner and his mother was enslaved) and during a portion of their escape he disguised himself as Rebecca's "owner".

They made their way all the way to Massachusetts. Unfortunately for George, he was spotted right away by someone who knew his former owner and in a short time he found himself in prison. George's owner came to Boston from Virginia and had George arrested for larceny (essentially saying that George stole himself).

As you may know, Massachusetts was a "hot bed" of abolitionist activity and when the word spread that George had been arrested, famous abolitionists like William Lloyd Garrison, and others, came to his defense. A journal was created, the Latimer Journal and North Star, which ran from November 11, 1842 - May 16, 1843.

Free African Americans also rose to support George— some three hundred African-American men came down to the courthouse where George was being kept and demanded that his owner not be allowed to do anything unlawful in his attempt to take George back to Virginia.

By this time Frederick Douglass was in New Bedford, Massachusetts and was active in the anti-slavery movement. He wrote his first public letter in support of George Latimer, in November of 1842. In his letter, which was published in The Liberator, Frederick Douglass highlighted the speeches he gave and the meetings he attended in support of George Latimer's case. He noted that he had never sought any publicity for his writings, but that this case was a special case. Douglass said that he could sympathize with George Latimer, because he too was cast into prison when he was suspected of trying to escape from Maryland.

Douglass resolved that he should do all that he was capable of doing for Latimer and that being in front of people…speaking with them and meeting with them…was where he could be effective.

This was where Douglass had a great impact—he could cause people to stop and think, because he knew about the realities of slavery and he powerfully presented arguments against it.

Not only Douglass, but many others rose to George

Latimer's defense. Thousands of people began to demand that Latimer be set free. In fact, after he was set free more than 65,000 people signed a petition, called the "Latimer Petition" (House No. 41, Commonwealth of Massachusetts in 1843), to request that the government of Massachusetts do the following...

1. "That a law should be passed, forbidding all persons who hold office under the government of Massachusetts from aiding in or abetting the arrest or detention of any person who may be claimed as a fugitive from slavery."

2. "That a law should be passed forbidding the use of the jails or other public property of the State, for the detention of any such person before described."

3. "That such amendments to the Constitution of the United States be proposed by the Legislature of Massachusetts to the other States of the Union, as may have the effect of forever separating the people of Massachusetts from all connection with slavery."

Of course the Constitution was not amended, as it relates to slavery, until after the Civil War began,...but the state of Massachusetts did respond by passing "AN ACT Further to protect Personal Liberty," which did address the first two points (but the impact of this law would be challenged by federal laws, such as the Fugitive Slave Act of 1850).

As for George Latimer, there was so much attention on his case that a deal was worked out (after court deliberations and the activism of many citizens) and an African-American reverend raised enough money to pay George's owner $400 for his emancipation.

Rebecca, during all this time, was hidden at a secret location. Her owner sent word that she would be taken back once George was sent back, but since George Latimer was freed, Rebecca's owner never tried to capture her and bring her back into slavery.

George and Rebecca were able to have their children, including Lewis Latimer, on free soil. If they had not had the courage to escape from slavery, Lewis Latimer might never have had the opportunity to make the contributions he did to the advancement of commercial lighting and toward the submission of the patent for the telephone!

14

BIDDY MASON: AN AMERICAN PIONEER

(A selection from volume 1)

Biddy Mason was born, enslaved, in Hancock, Georgia in 1818. Her owner, Robert Smith, later moved to Mississippi where he became acquainted with the Mormon religion. The mid-1800s were a tumultuous time in American politics and 1850 was an important year, in many ways.

Unbeknownst to Biddy Mason, decisions being made about California and Utah were about to have a significant impact on her life.

In Congress, the Compromise of 1850 allowed California to be admitted into the Union as a free state...it also amended the Fugitive Slave Act, ended the sale of slaves in Washington, D.C. and created the territorial governments of New Mexico and Utah.

The new territory in Utah was not a state, but it was assigned a governor to oversee its administrative duties. Brigham Young, the leader of the Later-day Saints (Mormon) Church, was appointed as the first governor of the territory of Utah. This decision made many people, who had converted to the Mormon faith, move to Utah to be closer to their leader and to the establishment of this new territory.

Robert Smith had already converted to Mormonism and, sometime before all of this happened, he moved himself, and the slaves he owned, to the territory of Utah.

The Trip

It was a two thousand-mile journey from Mississippi to Utah and, of course, it had to be done by wagon, horseback, and by foot. Biddy Mason was forced to go on this trip, with Robert Smith, and had several duties to perform along the way. Biddy also had daughters—one eleven years old, one four years old, and one under a year old. In addition to taking care of her daughters, Biddy had to herd the cattle throughout this long journey; she had to prepare meals; and she performed midwife duties.

Once they arrived in Utah, Robert Smith settled there for several years. He then decided to go to California to join a Mormon settlement in San Bernardino County; this was another six hundred-mile journey during which Biddy walked behind a train of wagons, while again herding cattle.

Once in California, Biddy Mason and some of the other slaves Robert Smith brought with him, befriended members of the free black community, there.

Robert Smith remained in California for four years, but

when he decided that he no longer wanted to live in California and that he wanted to move to Texas, free African-Americans came to the aid of Biddy and the others.

Robert Smith was stopped by the sheriff of Los Angeles, when he was on his way out of town, and was served with a writ of habeas corpus. The matter was reviewed in the U.S. District Court of the County of Los Angeles and the judge determined that the:

"..said persons of color are entitled to their freedom, and are free and cannot be held in slavery or involuntary servitude..."

...given that California was a free state.

Thus on January 19, 1856, Biddy Mason, her three children (Ellen, Ann and Harriet), and ten other people who were enslaved by Robert Smith were freed.

Her Work

Biddy Mason got a job as a midwife and nurse and began to save up her money. She eventually purchased property at 331 South Spring Street in what is now downtown Los Angeles. She was a smart woman and purchased additional properties, which grew in value as the city of Los Angeles grew.

For instance, she purchased and then reportedly sold one of her properties (a forty-foot lot) for $12,000, which was a considerable sum, as you can imagine, at that time. She amassed a great amount of wealth and her children and grandchildren also shared in her wisdom as they, too, managed the real estate that she gave them and sold their land for profits.

Biddy Mason became a well-known philanthropist. During a flood in the early 1880s, many people in the area lost their homes. Biddy contracted with a local grocery store and bought food for a good deal of the families who were made homeless by the flood. She also visited prisons and became known as Grandma Mason, in the community.

She helped to start the oldest African-American church in Los Angeles, the First African Methodist Episcopal Church in 1872. The church is still in existence today and has over 19,000 members.

Grandma Mason also operated one of the city's first day care centers and she opened her home to new settlers, who were in need of help, as they came to the city of Los Angeles.

Today, the location of her original home is a historic site in Los Angeles. Biddy Mason was an American pioneer.

15

CARTER G. WOODSON AND BLACK HISTORY MONTH

(A selection from volume 1)

Carter G. Woodson was born on December 19, 1875 in New Canton, VA.

His parents moved to Huntington, West Virginia where Woodson worked, as a young man. He spent six years digging and loading coal, in mines, along the New River Gorge in WV.

There he heard coal miners tell stories of their families and of their lives. He thought how amazing it was to hear stories of the past and about history. Hearing those miners intensified his interest in the history of black people.

As time went on, Woodson saved up enough money to go to school and, at the age of twenty, he began high school at one of the few schools available for African Americans— Douglass High School in West Virginia (which was named after Frederick Douglass).

He finished his studies in just two years and went on to Berea College in Kentucky.

His love of education led him to teach and to become the principal of his alma mater (Douglass High School). He also travelled abroad and became a school supervisor in the Philippines, from 1903 - 1907. He later attended the University of Chicago where he received a master's degree and he went on to receive a Ph.D., in history, in 1912 from Harvard University.

He continued to pursue a career in education and became dean of the School of Liberal Arts at Howard University and served as a dean of West Virginia State College.

Carter G. Woodson believed that the achievements of African Americans were grossly underrepresented and that there was a need to share their contributions. Woodson became a columnist for Marcus Garvey's weekly publication the Negro World and later went on to establish his own organization.

The Association for the Study of Negro Life and History

In 1915, he and Jesse E. Moorland founded the Association for the Study of Negro Life and History. This organization became a launching pad for the spreading of black history and in January of 1916 the first issue of the Journal of Negro History was published.

Woodson, and this organization, established Negro History Week in February of 1926.

This celebration would become Black History Month and it is now recognized as a time of reflection on the achievements of black people and African Americans, around the world.

In his lifetime, Carter G. Woodson contributed many scholarly works to the understanding of African-American achievements and experiences, including:

- The Education of the Negro Prior to 1861 (published in 1915)

- A Century of Negro Migration (1918)

- The History of the Negro Church (1921)

- The Negro in Our History (1922)

- The Mind of the Negro As Reflected in Letters Written During the Crisis 1800 - 1860 (published in 1926)

- African Myths: Together with Proverbs (1928)

- Negro Makers of History (1928, 1938, 1942)

- The Negro Wage Earner (published in 1930, along with Lorenzo Greene)

- **The Mis-Education of the Negro (1933)**

- The Story of the Negro Retold (1935)

Woodson believed that if the accomplishments of black people were properly set forth, it would show them as one of the makers of modern civilization and as factors in early human progress.

Carter G. Woodson

December 19, 1875 - April 3, 1950

16

CHARLES YOUNG AND THE BUFFALO SOLDIERS

Charles Young as a Captain in 1903.

Charles Young was a Buffalo Soldier, a pioneer in many ways, and one of the most celebrated African-American military men, at the time of his death.

He was born in 1864, in Kentucky, to Gabriel and Arminta Young. Gabriel and Arminta moved to Ripley, Ohio in 1866. Gabriel Young was a soldier in the Union Army during the Civil War and Charles grew up admiring his father's military background.

His mother encouraged him to excel academically and after being the first African American to graduate from his high school he took the advice of his parents and applied to the United States Military Academy at West Point. He experienced such discrimination that he later remarked that the worst thing he could wish for an enemy would be to make him a black man and send him to West Point.

He experienced racial harassment from instructors and his peers, but despite these challenges, he finished and became the third African American to graduate from West Point, in 1889.

There would not be another African American to complete West Point until 1936, 47 years later.

Buffalo Soldiers

African Americans were not allowed to join the Regular Army until after the Civil War—they fought and served in every American war from the American Revolution until the present day...they were simply not allowed to enlist in the Regular Army until after the Civil War.

At the conclusion of the Civil War, the U. S. needed soldiers to help rebuild the country and to patrol lands out west. So, in 1866, Congress created six segregated African-American regiments.

These regiments were eventually condensed into four units —they were the 9th and 10th Calvary and the 24th and 25th Infantry. Many of them were sent out West to patrol the Western Frontier, since more Americans started to settle in the West and conflicts with existing Native American nations arose. These soldiers served many roles:

- they protected Americans on the Western Frontier;

- guarded mail routes and escorted supply trains;

- built new roads;

- served in the Spanish-American War and in the Philippine-American War; and

- were among the first park rangers in our nation's history.

Native Americans (in particular the Cheyenne), out West, noted the fierce fighting abilities of theses soldiers and compared them to the buffalo. The buffalo was a well-respected figure in Native American culture and was seen as a fierce fighter. The term stuck and African Americans who served during this time period became known as "Buffalo Soldiers"!

Charles Young—A Buffalo Soldier

Charles Young left West Point and was commissioned as a second lieutenant in the Army. He served most of his active years with the Buffalo Soldiers in the 9th and 10th Calvary regiments.

He was assigned to regiments in Nebraska, Montana, and Utah. During the Spanish-American War he was assigned to the command of a National Guard battalion and temporarily given the rank of major. In 1899, he went overseas with the 9th Calvary to the Philippines and fought, there, for three years.

In 1902, upon returning to the U. S., Young was Captain of Company "I" of the 9th Calvary. He was stationed in San

Francisco, at the Presidio (or fortified military post) there. In 1903 Companies "I" and "M" escorted Theodore Roosevelt through San Francisco during his visit; which was the first time African-American soldiers served as the honor guard for a United States President.

Young was sent to Sequoia National Park, in the summer of 1903, because the Army was charged with the administration of several national parks before the creation of the National Park Service in 1916. Young and his soldiers built roads that extended access within the park. In his role, he became the first African-American Superintendent of a national park.

Charles Young and his soldiers built more miles of road, in that summer, than what had been built in the three previous summers, combined.

A Man of Determination

Young was also, in 1894, appointed as a Professor of Military Science and Tactics at Wilberforce University and the president of that college noted that he was "eminently qualified for the position...teaching not only Military Science courses, but also French and mathematics." There he met and befriended the famous sociologist, W. E. B. Du Bois.

Young continued to be awarded promotions—he served as the military attache' to Liberia and was a squadron commander in the Punitive Expedition against Pancho Villa in Mexico. Just prior to the beginning of World War I, Young was the highest ranking African-American officer in the U. S. Army.

As a part of his regular medical examinations, Young was diagnosed with nephritis (inflammation of the kidney), high blood pressure, and an enlarged heart. There was also pressure on the President of the United States and the Secretary of War not to let white soldiers serve under Charles Young's command.

In July of 1917 Young was medically retired and given the rank of Colonel in recognition of his distinguished service. Young was not happy—he was determined to prove he was fit for service.

He was 54 years old, at the time. Determined to demonstrate his fitness, he mounted a horse in Wilberforce, Ohio and rode 500 miles to Washington, D.C. He was granted an audience with the Secretary of War, but was not given a reversal of the decision. Despite being medically retired, he was kept on as an active duty officer and went on to train African-American servicemen.

Charles Young was a well-known figure and was seen as a highly respected and disciplined military leader. He died while on a military attache' mission in 1922, in Africa, and was buried in Arlington National Cemetery, in 1923.

In an incredible show of respect, he was the fourth soldier, ever, to be honored with a funeral service at the Arlington Memorial Amphitheater, in Arlington National Cemetery.

Arlington Memorial Amphitheater.

REFERENCES AND IMAGES

Cover: Frederick Douglass, NPS, National Historical Site, FRDO 3936; Sojourner Truth, Library of Congress, LC-USZ62-119343; & Harriet Tubman, Library of Congress, Lindsley, H. B., photographer.

Chapter 1: Henry Johnson and the Harlem Hellfighters

References:

Four Centuries of Service, The National Guard Celebrates its African-American Heritage. Accessed 8-2015.

National Archives. *Teaching with Documents: Photographs of the 369th Infantry and African Americans during World War I.* Accessed 8-2015.

The White House. Office of the Press Secretary, *President Obama to Award Medal of Honor.* May 14, 2015, accessed June 2015.

Sergeant Henry Johnson: Medal of Honor. Army.mil Features. Accessed 8-2015.

Vergun, David. U.S. Army. *Harlem Hellfighter's valor in battle inspires Americans.* Accessed 8-2015.

Photos:

Sgt. Henry Johnson of the 369th Infantry Regiment was awarded the French Croix de Guerre for bravery during an outnumbered battle with German soldiers, Feb. 12, 1919. This photo, from Feb. 12, 1919, was taken just before his discharge from the Army. U.S. Army (Photo: Public Domain)

New York Division of Military and Naval Affairs. Sgt. Henry Johnson and the Harlem Hellfighters' parade is shown as it passes through New York during February 1919.

Arlington National Cemetery, Red and Black Ink, LLC. 2015.

New York's famous 369th regiment arrives home from France, National Archives and Records Administration, Records of the War Department, Record Group 165, National Archives Identifier: 533548.

Chapter 2: Charles Ball

References:

Ball, Charles. *Fifty Years in Chains or the Life of an American Slave.* New York: H. Dayton, 1858.

Ball, Charles. *Slavery in the United States: A Narrative of the Life and Adventures of Charles Ball.* New York: John S. Taylor, 1837.

LeMaster, J. R. and James Wilson, editors and Christie Hamric, research. *The Mark Twain Encyclopedia*, 1993. *Ball, Charles* by Howard G. Baetzhold, pages 61 and 62.

Smith, Gene Allen. *American liberty and slavery in the Chesapeake: The paradox of Charles Ball.* Fighting for Freedom: African Americans in the War of 1812, NPS, accessed 9-2015.

The War of 1812. *Black Sailors and Soldiers in the War of 1812*, PBS. Accessed 9-2015.

Photos:

Fort McHenry National Monument and Historic Shrine, Red and Black Ink, LLC. 2015.

Chapter 3: Ethel Waters: A Remarkable Career

References:

Academy Awards (22nd), 1950. Academy of Motion Picture Arts and Sciences, Actress in a Supporting Role, Ethel Waters, Pinky. Accessed 8-2015. http://www.oscars.org/oscars/ceremonies/1950

Armstrong, Robin. *"Waters, Ethel 1895–1977."* Contemporary Black Biography. 1994. Accessed August 17, 2015 from Encyclopedia.com: http://www.encyclopedia.com/doc/1G2-2870900074.html

B'Way, *Broadway the American Musical: Ethel Waters.* PBS. Thirteen/WNET New York. http://www.pbs.org/wnet/broadway/stars/ethel-waters/

Chester's Influence on American Music: Ethel Waters. Industrial Heritage Parkway, Delaware County, PA. Accessed 8-2015. http://www.co.delaware.pa.us/planning/environmental/IHPSignage/ChestersInfluenceonAmericanMusic.pdf

Biographies: *Ethel Waters.* JAZZ, PBS Online. New Grove Dictionary of Jazz. Oxford University Press. Accessed 8-2015. http://www.pbs.org/jazz/biography/artist_id_waters_ethel.htm

Grammy Hall of Fame. The Recording Academy. https://www.grammy.org/recording-academy/awards/hall-of-fame#d

Hutchisson, James. *"DuBose Heyward: A Charleston Gentleman and the World of Porgy and Bess."* University Press of Mississippi, 2000.

NBCUniversal: Our History. Accessed 8-2015. http://www.nbcuniversal.com/our-history

Television Academy. Ethel Waters: Awards and Nominations, Outstanding Single Performance by an Actress in a Leading Role - 1962. Accessed 8-2015.

Waters, Ethel with Charles Samuels. *His Eye in on the Sparrow: An Autobiography,* 1951. Cambridge: De Capo Press Addition, 1992.

Photos:

Ethel Waters, William Gotlieb Collection, Library of Congress, LC-GLB23-0891 DLC.

Piano in Black and White, Red and Black Ink, LLC. 2015.

Chapter 4: Ida B. Wells and Why She Began to Write

References:

PBS. *The Rise and Fall of Jim Crow: Ida B. Wells (1862 - 1931).* Educational Broadcasting Company, accessed March 2015.

Wells, Ida B., Edited by Duster, Alfreda M. *Crusade for Justice, The Autobiography of Ida B. Wells.* Chicago: The University of Chicago Press, 1970.

Wells, Ida B., *Southern Horrors: Lynch Law in All Its Phases. New York Age, print,* 1892.

Photos:

Ida B. Wells from the *Afro-American Press and Its Editors,* 1891.

Railroad tracks, Red and Black Ink, LLC, 2015.

Chapter 5: Harriet Tubman: The Combahee River Raid

References:

Bradford, Sarah. *Harriet Tubman, The Moses of Her People.* New York: G. R. Lockwood and Son, 1886.

Braford, Sarah. *Scenes in the Life of Harriet Tubman.* Auburn: W. J. Moses, 1869.

Central Intelligence Agency. *Intelligence in the Civil War: Black Dispatches.* https://www.cia.gov/library/publications/additional-publications/civil-war/p20.htm, accessed October 2013.

National Archives. *Claim of Harriet Tubman and Lesson Plans: Congress and Harriet Tubman's Claim for a Pension.* http://www.archives.gov/legislative/resources/education/tubman/all-lesson-materials.pdf http://www.archives.gov/legislative/features/claim-of-harriet-tubman/, accessed October 2013.

South Carolina General Assembly, 120th Session, 2013 - 2014. Resolution 4236, Sponsored by Representative Hodges. http://scstatehouse.gov/sess120_2013-2014/bills/4236.htm, accessed October 2013.

Photos:

Harriet Tubman, full-length portrait, Lindsley, H. B., photographer. Courtesy National Park Service

Chapter 6: Frederick Douglass: How He Learned to Read and Write

References:

Douglass, Frederick. *Narrative of the Life of Frederick Douglass.* Published at the Anti-Slavery Office, No 25 Cornhill, 1845.

Douglass, Frederick. *My Bondage and My Freedom.* New York, 1855.

Smith, Danita. *We Were Heroes: Frederick Douglass and Harriet Tubman.* Maryland: Red and Black Ink, LLC, 2014.

Photos:

Frederick Douglass National Historic Site, FRDO 3925, courtesy National Park Service.

Chapter 7: Sojourner Truth and Her Famous Lawsuit

References:

Gilbert, Olive. *Narrative of Sojourner Truth,* 1850.

New York State Archives. AN ACT relative to slaves and servants. http://iarchives.nysed.gov/dmsBlue/viewImageData.jsp?id=177899

Photos:

Photo: Library of Congress, Sojourner Truth, three-quarter length portrait, standing, wearing spectacles, shawl, and peaked cap, right hand resting on cane, Date Created/Published: [Detroit], [1864]. Reproduction Number: LC-USZ62-119343 (b&w film copy neg.)

Chapter 8: Phillis Wheatley: An Example of Erudition

References:

American Treasures of the Library of Congress. *A Voice of Her Own. Phillis Wheatley.* Accessed 4-2014. http://www.loc.gov/exhibits/treasures/ tri013.html, Accessed 4-2014. http://www.medfordhistorical.org/ medford-history/africa-to-medford/tomothy-fitch/

Massachusetts Historical Society. *African Americans and the End of Slavery. Phillis Wheatley.* Accessed 4-2014. http://www.masshist.org/endofslavery/ index.php?id=57

America's Story from America's Library. *Phillis Wheatley, the First African American Published Book of Poetry, September 1, 1773.* Accessed 4-2014. http://www.americaslibrary.gov/jb/revolut/jb_revolut_poetslav_1.html

African American Odyssey. *Individual Accomplishments: Phillis Wheatley's Love of Freedom.* Accessed 4-2014. http://memory.loc.gov/ammem/aaohtml/ exhibit/aopart2.html#0215

Wheatley, Phillis. *Poems on Various Subjects, Religious and Moral, 1773.* Rare Book and Special Collections Division, Library of Congress.

Photos:

Wheatley, Phillis. *Poems on Various Subjects, Religious and Moral, 1773.* Rare Book and Special Collections Division, Library of Congress.

Chapter 9: Benjamin Banneker: A Renaissance Man and an Abolitionist

References:

Benjamin Banneker Historical Park and Museum. Friends of Benjamin Banneker Historical Park and Museum, Oella, Maryland, 2015.

Declaring Independence: Drafting the Documents. Library of Congress, http://www.loc.gov/exhibits/declara/declara4.html, accessed 7-2015.

Jefferson Responds to Banneker. American Treasures of the Library of Congress. http://www.loc.gov/exhibits/treasures/trr022.html, accessed 7-2015.

Mathematician and Astronomer Benjamin Banneker Was Born November 9, 1731. America's Story from America's Library. http://www.americaslibrary.gov/jb/colonial/jb_colonial_banneker_1.html, accessed 7-2015.

Tyson, Martha Ellicott (1795 - 1873), *A Sketch of the Life of Benjamin Banneker; from notes taken in 1836.* Maryland Historical Society, 1854, read by J. Saurin Norris, before the MHS, October 5, 1854.

Photos:

Benjamin Banneker's Pennsylvania, Delaware, Maryland and Virginia Almanack and Ephemeris, for the Year of Our Lord 1792. Created and published in Baltimore: William Goddard and James Angell, 1791. Library of Congress Rare Book and Special Collections Division. Digital ID, rbcmisc ody0214.

Chapter 10: Beginnings of the African Methodist Episcopal Church

References:

Allen, Richard. *The Life and Gospel Labors of the Rt. Rev. Richard Allen.* Philadelphia: Martin & Boston, 1833.

Mother Bethel African Methodist Episcopal Church. *Church History*, accessed 6-2015.

The African Episcopal Church of St. Thomas, website. *About Absalom Jones,* accessed 6-2015.

Wright, Richard and Hawkins, J.R. *Centennial Encylcopedia of the African Methodist Episcopal Church.* Philadelphia: Book Concern of the A.M.E. Church, 1916.

Photos:

Bible. Red and Black Ink, LLC, 2015.

Chapter 11: History of Hilton Head and Mitchelville During the Civil War

References:

Finding Freedom's Home: Archaeology at Mitchelville. Accessed 11-2015.
 http://www.bcgov.net/mitchelville/

Gulla Geechee Cultural Heritage Corridor.   Our History and Culture.
Accessed 11-2015. http://gullahgeecheecorridor.org

Photos:

Map of South Carolina. U. S. Geological Survey, National Atlas.

Sunset. Red and Black Ink, LLC, 2015.

Chapter 12: William Jones and His Escape

References:

Still, William. *The Underground Railroad.* Philadelphia: Porter & Coates, 1872.

Photos:

Harbor in Baltimore. Red and Black Ink, LLC, 2015.

Chapter 13: Lewis Latimer: Inventor, Draftsman and Electrical Engineer

References:

California Energy Commission.   Super Scientists: Lewis H. Latimer, accessed September 2014. http://www.energyquest.ca.gov/scientists/latimer.html.

George, Luvenia. Smithsonian Institution, Innovative Lives: Lewis Latimer (1848 - 1928), Renaissance Man, accessed September 2014.

Joint Special Committee of the Senate and House of Representatives of the State of Massachusetts on the Petition of George Latimer and Others. House, No. 41, Commonwealth of Massachusetts, General Court, 1843.

National Park Service.   Frederick Douglass Historic Site, Frederick Douglass Chronology, accessed March 2015.

National Park Service. Thomas Edison National Historic Park: A Few Gifted Men Who Worked for Edison, accessed September 2014.

Rutgers, The State University of New Jersey.   Queens Borough Public Library. Edited by: Janet M. Schneider and Bayla Singer. Edison Papers.

Blueprint for Change: The Life and Times of Lewis H. Latimer was organized by the Queens Borough Public Library and presented as an exhibition from February 3 through 8/26/1995. The State University of New Jersey.   Queens Borough Public Library. Edited by: Janet M. Schneider and Bayla Singer. Edison Papers, accessed September 2014.

The Library of Congress, THOMAS. Bills, Resolutions: H.CON.RES.252 -- Expressing the sense of the Congress that a postage stamp should be issued to recognize the achievements of Lewis Howard Latimer. (Introduced in House - IH), accessed September 2014.

The Library of Congress, THOMAS, Congressional Record: INTRODUCTION OF A RESOLUTION EXPRESSING THE SENSE OF CONGRESS THAT THE U.S. POSTAL SERVICE SHOULD ISSUE A STAMP COMMEMORATING LEWIS HOWARD LATIMER -- HON. FLOYD H. FLAKE (Extension of Remarks - May 25, 1994), accessed September 2014.

Photos:

Lewis Latimer, Courtesy NPS - Thomas Edison National Historic Park.

Chapter 14: Biddy Mason: An American Pioneer

References:

Beasley, Delilah. *The Negro Trail Blazers of California*. Los Angeles, CA: 1919.

First African Methodist Episcopal Church of Los Angeles, http://www.famechurch.org, accessed February 2014.

Library of Congress. Primary Documents in American History. *The Compromise of 1850.* http://www.loc.gov/rr/program/bib/ourdocs/Compromise1850.html, accessed February 2014.

National Park Service. A History of Black Americans in California: HISTORIC SITES, http://www.cr.nps.gov/history/online_books/5views/5views2h14.htm, accessed February 2014.

Dr. Taylor, Quintard, Scott and Dorothy Bullitt, Professor of American History, Primary Documents: MASON v. SMITH (THE BRIDGET "BIDDY" MASON CASE), 1856, http://faculty.washington.edu/qtaylor/documents_us/mason_v_smith.htm, accessed February 2014.

USC Dornsife, College of Letters, Arts, and Sciences. Downtown Los Angeles Walking Tour. Biddy Mason Park, Broadway and Spring Street, between 3rd and 4th street http://dornsife.usc.edu/la-walking-tour/biddy-mason-park/, accessed February 2014.

Utah Division of State History. Utah's Territorial Governors (1850-1896), http://www.ilovehistory.utah.gov/people/difference/territorial_govs.html, accessed February 2014.

Photos:

Biddy Mason from, *The Negro Trail Blazers of California.*

Chapter 15: Carter G. Woodson and Black History Month

References:

Brown, Korey. *Carter G. Woodson.* Association for the Study of African American Life and History. http://asalh.org/woodsonbiosketch.html, accessed January 2014.

Hosted by the Library of Congress. African American History Month: Profiles, Carter G. Woodson.
http://www.africanamericanhistorymonth.gov/woodson.html, accessed January 2014.

National Park Service, Carter G. Woodson Home. National Historical Site, District of Columbia. http://www.nps.gov/cawo/index.htm, accessed January 2014.

National Park Service, National River. New River Gorge, West Virginia.
http://www.nps.gov/neri/historyculture/carter-g-woodson.htm, accessed January 2014

Photos:

Photo Courtesy of the National Park Service, Carter G. Woodson Home. National Historical Site.

Chapter 16: Charles Young and the Buffalo Soldiers

References:

Charles Young Buffalo Soldiers National Monument, Ohio. *History and Culture: Charles Young.* http://www.nps.gov/chyo/historyculture/index.htm, accessed January 2014.

National Park Service. Presidio of San Francisco, California. *Buffalo Soldiers.* http://www.nps.gov/prsf/historyculture/buffalo-soldiers.htm, accessed January 2014.

National Park Service. Presidio of San Francisco, California. *Charles Young-Leader of Men.* http://www.nps.gov/prsf/historyculture/charles-young-leader-of-men.htm, accessed January 2014.

Presidential Proclamation - Charles Young Buffalo Soldiers National Monument. March 25, 2013. The White House. Office of the Press Secretary. http://www.whitehouse.gov/the-press-office/2013/03/25/presidential-proclamation-charles-young-buffalo-soldiers-national-monume, accessed January 2014.

Sequoia and Kings Canyon National Park, California. National Park Service, Charles Young. http://home.nps.gov/seki/historyculture/young.htm, accessed January 2014.

Photos:

Charles Young as a Captain in 1903 U.S. Center of Military History.

Golden Gate Bridge. Red and Black Ink, LLC, 2015.

Sunset in the road. Red and Black Ink, LLC, 2015.

Arlington Memorial Amphitheater. Red and Black Ink, LLC, 2015.

ABOUT US

Red and Black Ink, LLC is dedicated to growth through education and history. Our mission is to help parents play an active role in the educational development of their children and to help children achieve educational success!

Danita Smith is the founder of Red and Black Ink, LLC. She writes about history and education from the perspective of real life—as a person who has graduated from public schools, obtained her bachelor's degree in business administration, obtained her M.B.A. from an HBCU and secured employment in a STEM-related field for more than 20 years. During that time she was a corporate trainer, a business manager and a hiring manager, which required extensive knowledge of disease states, quantitative methods and scientific applications. She hopes her real-world experiences as a mother, a student, an author, a hiring manager and an entrepreneur will help others as they seek to ensure the academic growth of their children.

Please visit our website: **BlackandEducation.com**

Red and Black Ink

www.ingramcontent.com/pod-product-compliance
Lightning Source LLC
Chambersburg PA
CBHW070814050426
42452CB00011B/2039